SAURUS

Claire Freedman and Ben Cort

Sandy Creek
NEW YORK

With much love to Paul,
Jacquie, Liam, and Nushy — CF

For Johnny and Anna,
with all my love — BC

An Imprint of Sterling Publishing
387 Park Avenue South
New York, NY 10016

SANDY CREEK and the distinctive Sandy Creek logo are registered trademarks of Barnes & Noble, Inc.

Text © 2011 by Claire Freedman
Illustrations © 2011 by Ben Cort

First published in Great Britain in 2011 by Simon & Schuster UK Ltd
This 2013 edition published by Sandy Creek.

ISBN 978-1-4351-4952-6

Manufactured in China
Lot #:
2 4 6 8 10 9 7 5 3 1
04/13

Monty **LOVES** inventing,

BUT things don't always work . . .

One day Monty found a book:

INVENTIONS VERY RARE!

CREATE YOURSELF A MONSTER FRIEND BUT ONLY IF YOU DARE!

The book said:

TAKE SOME BRIGHT GREEN SLIME,
A SOCK—PREFERABLY SMELLY,
HEAT TO A GOO WITH MOLDY CHEESE,
STIR IN SOME STRAWBERRY JELLY!

WHOOSH!

Bright sparks flashed,
Out shot a **THING . . .**

All swampy, green, and wobbly.
"I'M BOGABLOB!"
the monster drooled.

Monty grabbed the book again:

TAKE SAWDUST — JUST A PUFF,
HEAT WITH A CAN OF REFRIED BEANS,
ADD BELLY-BUTTON FLUFF.

"Eww!" Monty gulped and held his nose.
"This mixture smells so weird!"

THEN . . .

POOOOF!

An even crazier THING . . .

A **DUST MONSTER** appeared!

"HEY, BOGABLOB!" Dust Monster roared, "Let's have a MONSTER FIGHT!"

KAPOW!

went Monty's formula,

And from the fizzing mix . . .

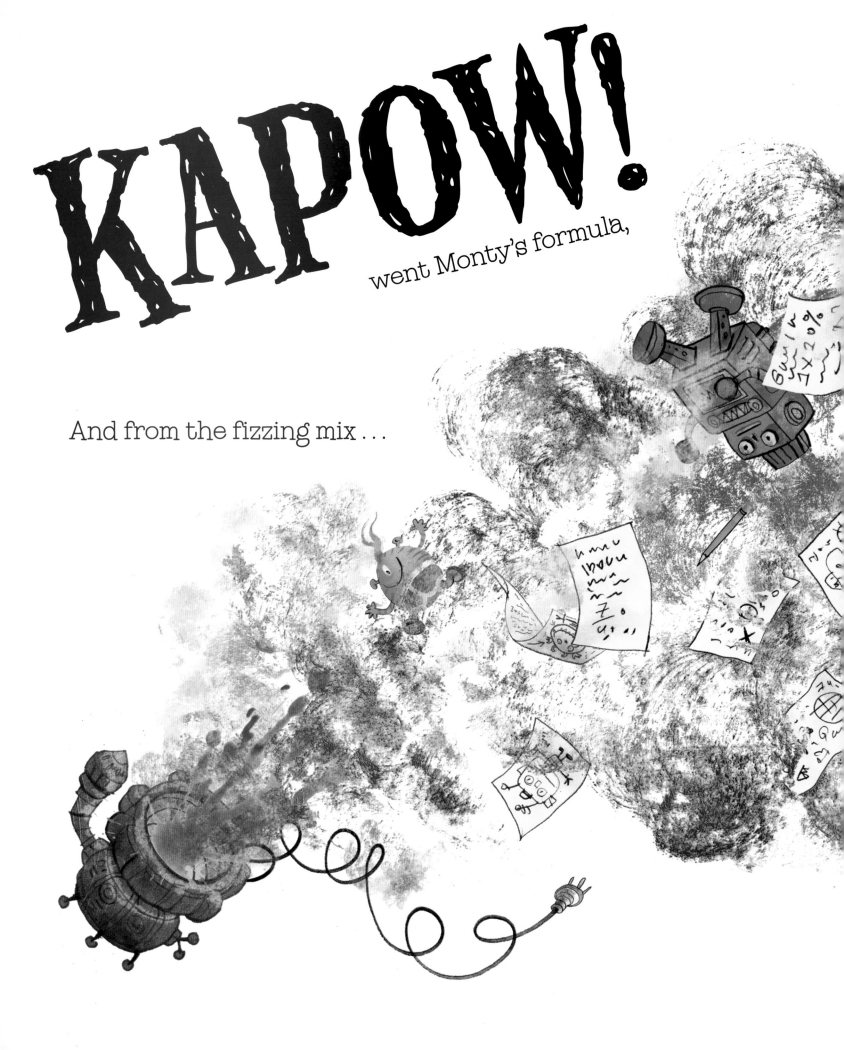

Burst big, bad **MONSTERSAURUS** "I'll sort your monster fix!"

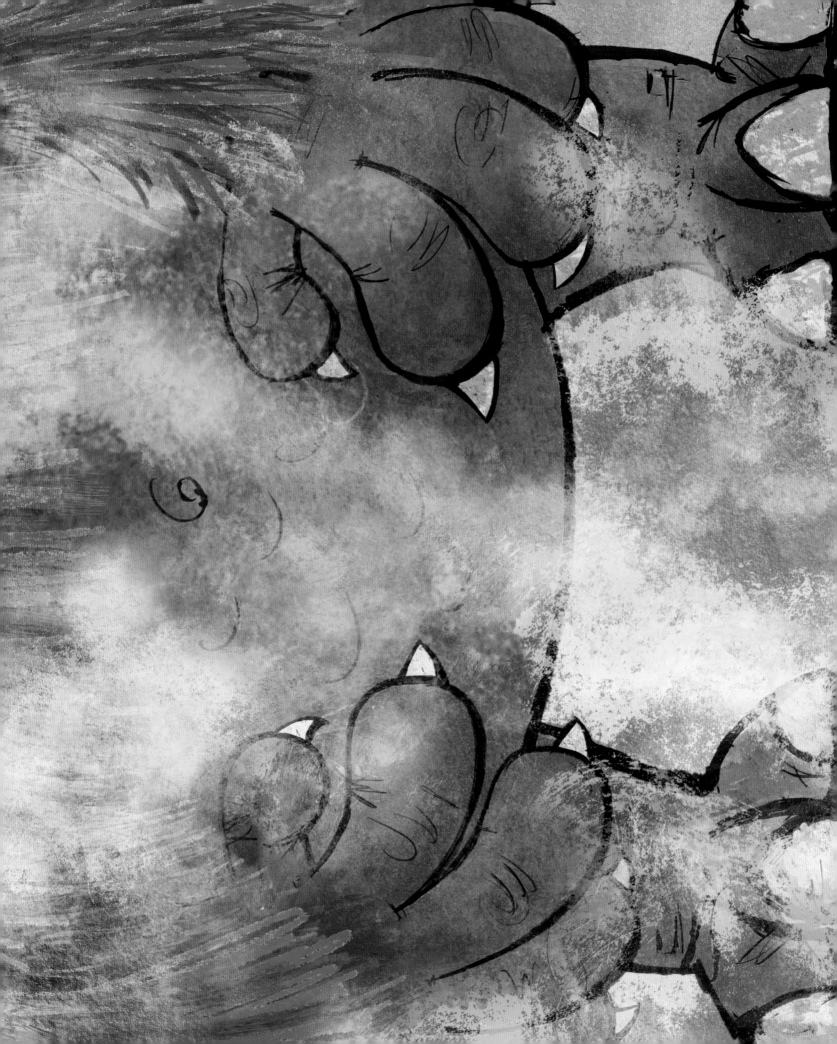

GRRRR!
Monstersaurus roared a ROAR,
And hissed a horrid HISS.

"Get lost, you measly monsters,
Or you'll get a GREAT
BIG ..."

"KISS!"

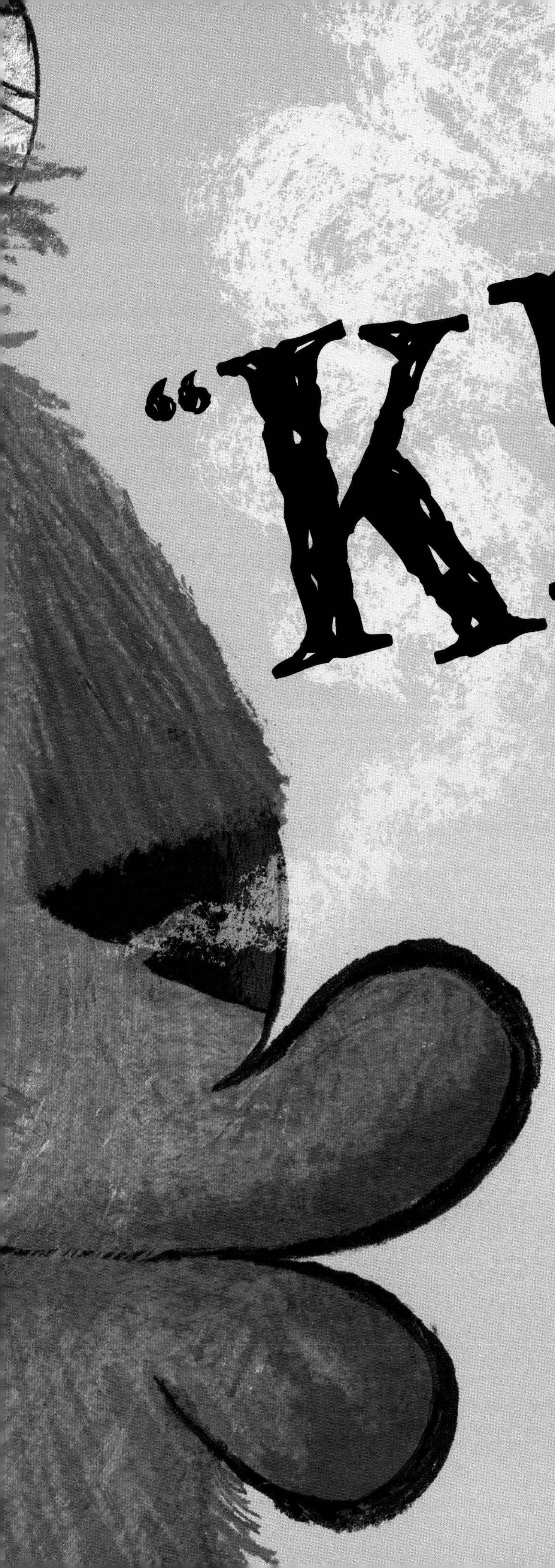

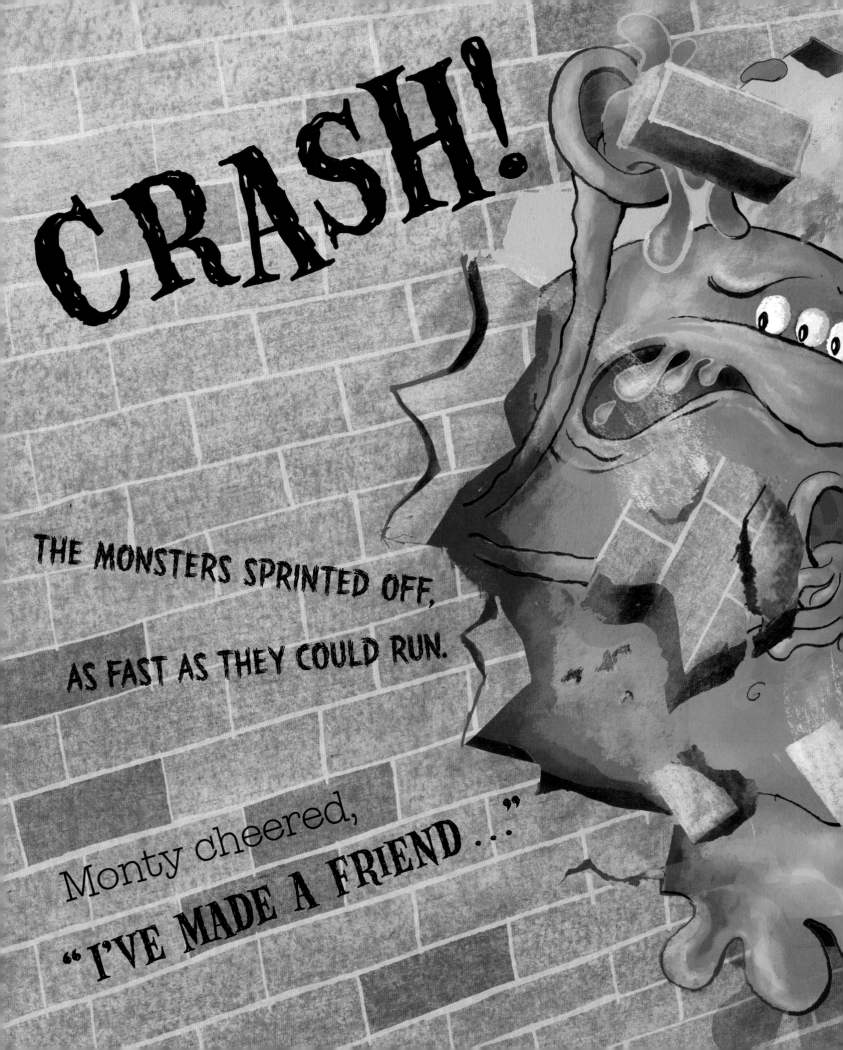

CRASH!

THE MONSTERS SPRINTED OFF,

AS FAST AS THEY COULD RUN.

Monty cheered,

"I'VE MADE A FRIEND . . ."

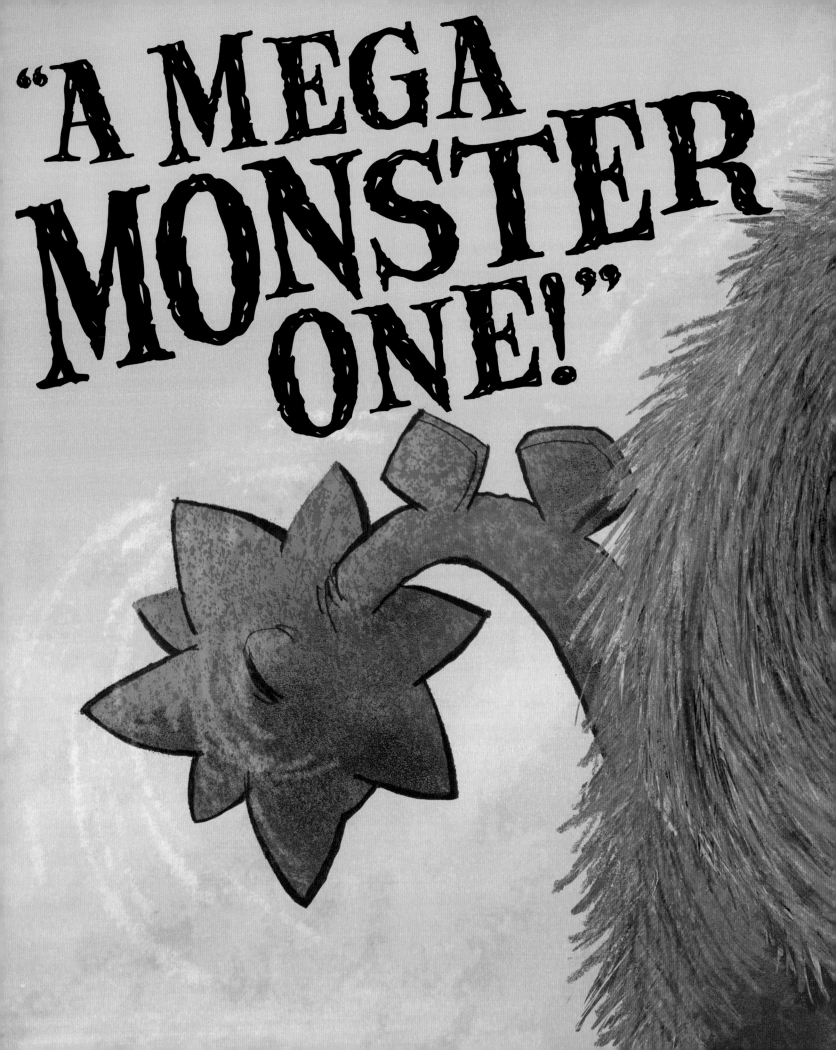

Said Monty to his new best friend,
"It's great–just you and me!"
What fun did they get up to?

YOU'LL HAVE TO WAIT AND SEE . . .